# YOU CAN DRAW IT!

# ROBOTS

WRITTEN BY MAGGIE ROSIER
CONCEPTS AND ILLUSTRATIONS
BY STEVE PORTER

BELLWETHER MEDIA · MINNEAPOLIS, MN

This edition first published in 2013 by Bellwether Media, Inc.

Library of Congress Cataloging-in-Publication Data

Rosier, Maggie.
  Robots / by Maggie Rosier.
    pages cm. – (Express: you can draw it!)
  Includes bibliographical references and index.
  Summary: "Information accompanies step-by-step instructions on how to draw robots. The text level and subject matter
are intended for students in grades 3 through 7"–Provided by publisher.
  ISBN 978-1-60014-900-9 (hardcover : alk. paper)
  1. Robots in art–Juvenile literature. 2. Drawing–Technique–Juvenile literature. I. Title.
  NC825.R56R67 2013
  743'.89629892–dc23
                          2012044024

Printed in the United States of America, North Mankato, MN.

# TABLE OF CONTENTS

# ROBOTS!

Most people think of robots as **humanoids** that function on their own. However, most real-life robots are simply machines that do work for humans. There is no telling what kinds of **automatons** will exist in the future. For now, we can only imagine the forms they will take!

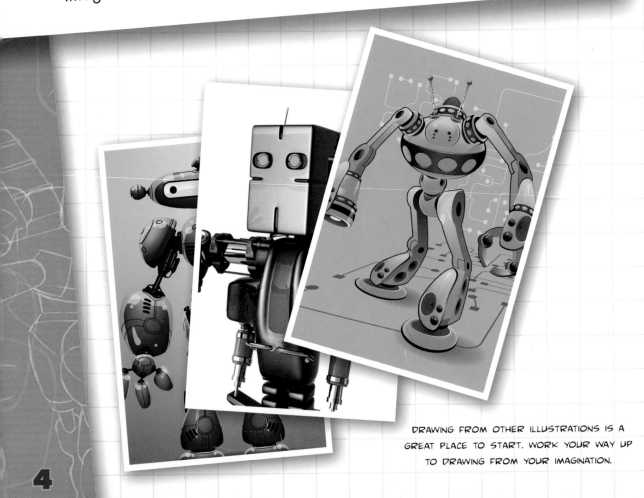

DRAWING FROM OTHER ILLUSTRATIONS IS A GREAT PLACE TO START. WORK YOUR WAY UP TO DRAWING FROM YOUR IMAGINATION.

Before you begin drawing, you will need a few basic supplies.

PAPER

DRAWING
PENCILS

## 2B OR NOT 2B?

NOT ALL DRAWING PENCILS ARE THE SAME. "B" PENCILS ARE SOFTER, MAKE DARKER MARKS, AND SMUDGE EASILY. "H" PENCILS ARE HARDER, MAKE LIGHTER MARKS, AND DON'T SMUDGE VERY MUCH AT ALL.

BLACK INK
PEN

COLORED PENCILS
(ALL DRAWINGS IN THIS BOOK WERE FINISHED WITH COLORED PENCILS.)

ERASER

PENCIL
SHARPENER

# Crush
## The Recycling Robot

Crush works for the environment. This recycling machine can be found digging through junkyards and trash dumps. Giant **tracks** take Crush over hills and through ditches to collect items that can be reused. Powerful pincers break vehicles down into usable scraps. When Crush is around, nothing goes to waste.

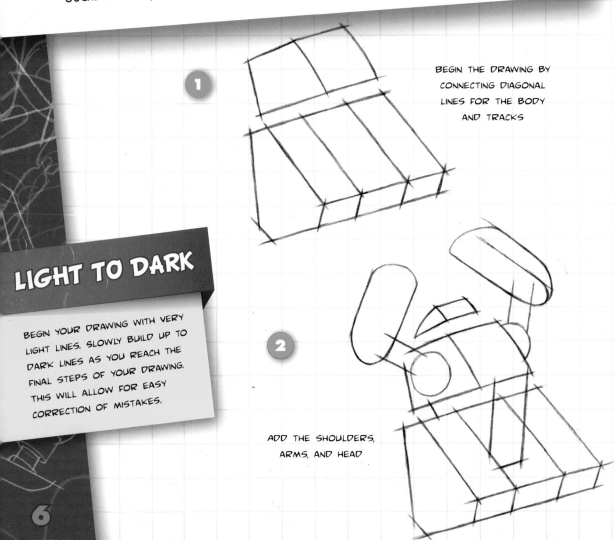

**1**

BEGIN THE DRAWING BY CONNECTING DIAGONAL LINES FOR THE BODY AND TRACKS

## LIGHT TO DARK

BEGIN YOUR DRAWING WITH VERY LIGHT LINES. SLOWLY BUILD UP TO DARK LINES AS YOU REACH THE FINAL STEPS OF YOUR DRAWING. THIS WILL ALLOW FOR EASY CORRECTION OF MISTAKES.

**2**

ADD THE SHOULDERS, ARMS, AND HEAD

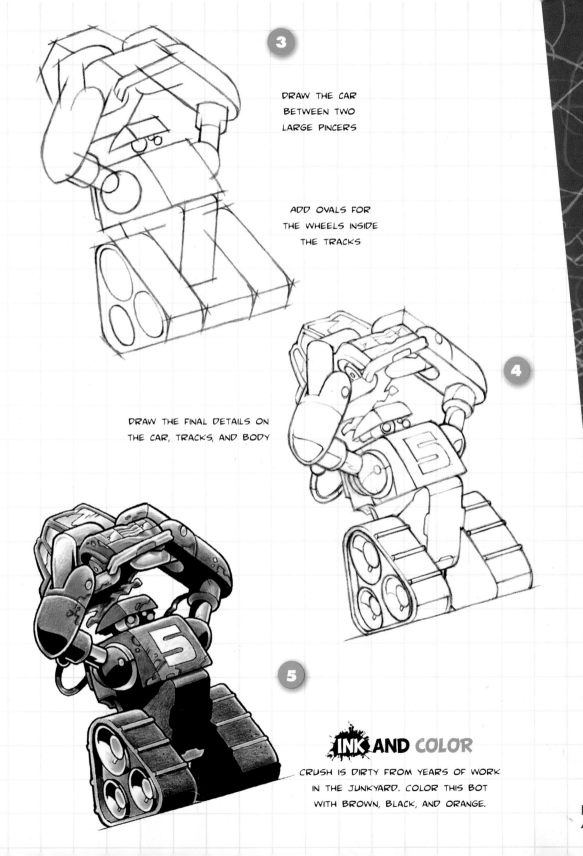

**3**

DRAW THE CAR
BETWEEN TWO
LARGE PINCERS

ADD OVALS FOR
THE WHEELS INSIDE
THE TRACKS

DRAW THE FINAL DETAILS ON
THE CAR, TRACKS, AND BODY

**4**

**5**

# INK AND COLOR

CRUSH IS DIRTY FROM YEARS OF WORK
IN THE JUNKYARD. COLOR THIS BOT
WITH BROWN, BLACK, AND ORANGE.

**7**

# Raze
## The All-In-One Demolisher

Meet the ultimate destroyer. Raze is taking over **demolition** sites by performing tasks normally done by multiple machines. A **wrecking ball** arm brings brick tumbling to the ground. The other arm is equipped with fingers to sift through the **rubble**. The tallest building has nothing on Raze.

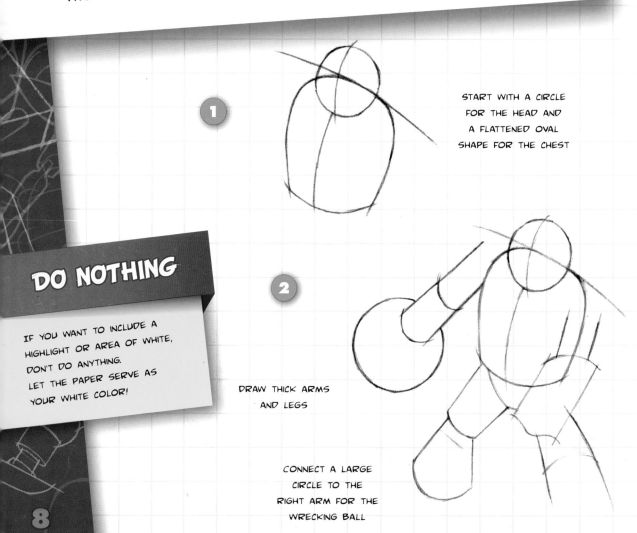

**1** START WITH A CIRCLE FOR THE HEAD AND A FLATTENED OVAL SHAPE FOR THE CHEST

**2** DRAW THICK ARMS AND LEGS

CONNECT A LARGE CIRCLE TO THE RIGHT ARM FOR THE WRECKING BALL

## DO NOTHING

IF YOU WANT TO INCLUDE A HIGHLIGHT OR AREA OF WHITE, DON'T DO ANYTHING. LET THE PAPER SERVE AS YOUR WHITE COLOR!

ADD THE FACIAL
FEATURES

**3**

USE BOXY SHAPES
TO SECTION OFF THE
SHOULDERS, CHEST,
AND STOMACH

ADD FOUR FINGERS TO
THE LEFT HAND

**4**

ADD HOSES, DIRT, AND
OTHER FINISHING TOUCHES

**5**

INK AND COLOR

THIS DESTRUCTIVE MACHINE IS
COLORED YELLOW TO MATCH
OTHER HEAVY MACHINERY.
SHADING AND HIGHLIGHTS MAKE
RAZE POP OFF THE PAGE.

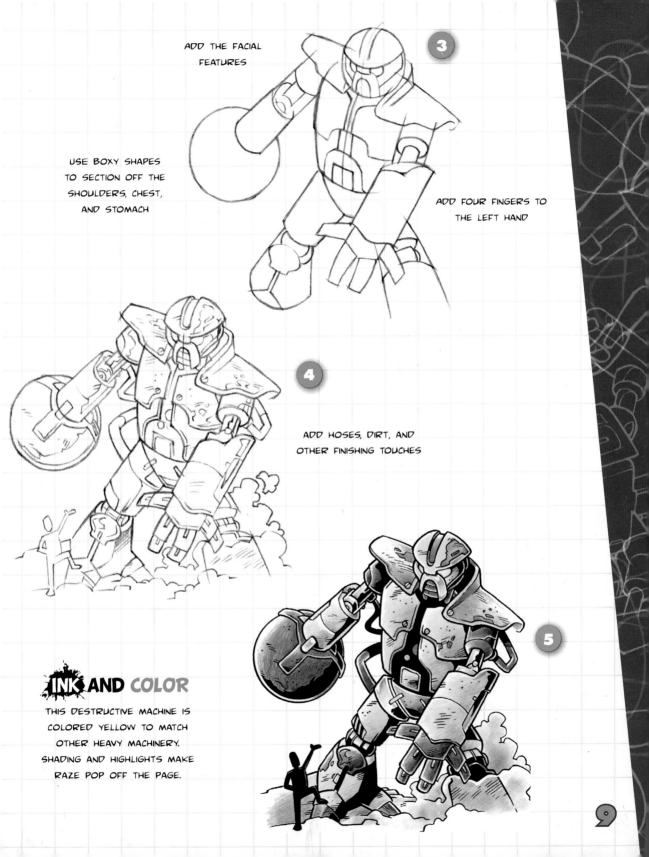

# D-Buggr
## The Doctor's Little Helper

D-Buggr goes where no surgeon has gone before. This **microscopic** bot is small enough to surf through your bloodstream and stop off at every **vital** organ. On its way, it unclogs **arteries** and destroys unhealthy cells. After a trip through your system, D-Buggr will know you inside out!

## USE YOUR ARM

DRAW WITH YOUR WHOLE ARM, NOT JUST YOUR WRIST AND FINGERS.

**1**

BEGIN WITH A LARGE OVAL FOR THE BODY

USE FOUR HALF-CIRCLES TO MARK WHERE THE ARMS AND LEGS WILL ATTACH

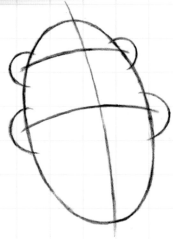

**2**

ADD THE FIRST SECTIONS OF THE ARMS AND LEGS

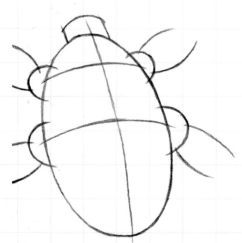

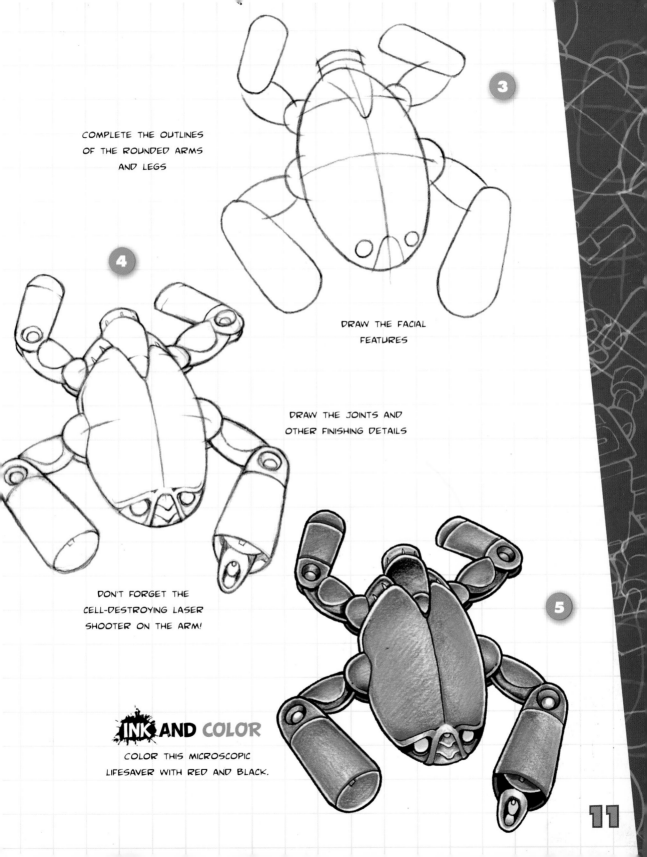

COMPLETE THE OUTLINES
OF THE ROUNDED ARMS
AND LEGS

3

DRAW THE FACIAL
FEATURES

4

DRAW THE JOINTS AND
OTHER FINISHING DETAILS

DON'T FORGET THE
CELL-DESTROYING LASER
SHOOTER ON THE ARM!

5

INK AND COLOR

COLOR THIS MICROSCOPIC
LIFESAVER WITH RED AND BLACK.

# Point
## The One-Bot Rescue Force

Despite its name, Point doesn't have a single edge on its frame. Its flexible build and ability to see in every direction make Point the perfect partner in a dangerous situation. A 50-foot (15-meter) hose that extends from its back can put out fires, vacuum up troublemakers, and lasso victims to safety!

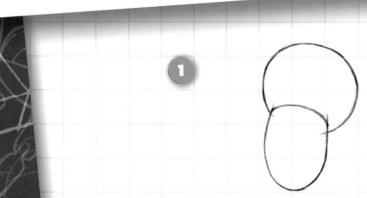

**1** BEGIN WITH A CIRCLE CONNECTED TO A FLATTENED OVAL FOR THE BODY

ADD OVALS FOR THE UPPER SECTIONS OF THE ARMS AND LEGS

## SHINE ON

YOU CAN ADD HIGHLIGHTS OR REFLECTIONS TO A SURFACE TO MAKE IT LOOK SHINY. DO THIS BY FADING YOUR COLOR FROM VERY RICH TO THE WHITE OF THE PAPER.

**2**

DRAW THE FLAT HEAD

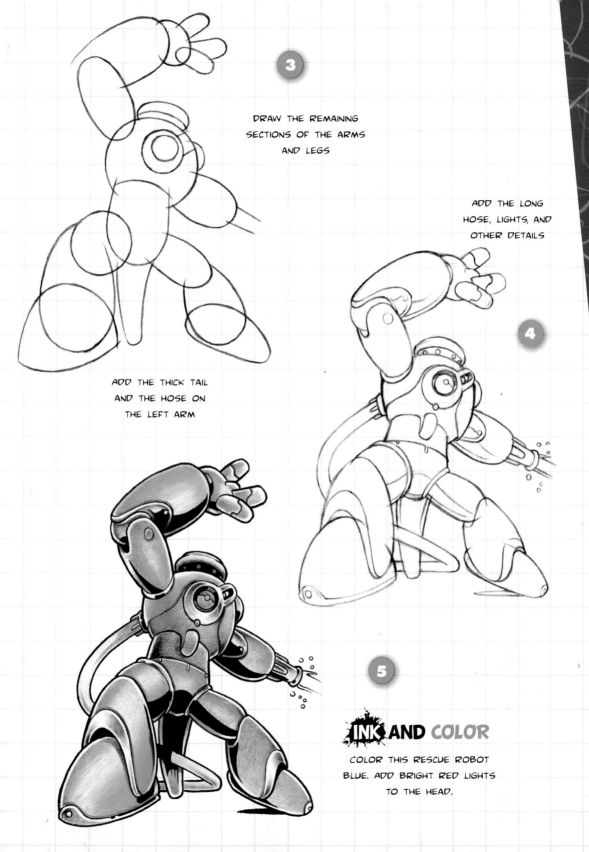

**3**

DRAW THE REMAINING
SECTIONS OF THE ARMS
AND LEGS

ADD THE LONG
HOSE, LIGHTS, AND
OTHER DETAILS

**4**

ADD THE THICK TAIL
AND THE HOSE ON
THE LEFT ARM

**5**

INK AND COLOR

COLOR THIS RESCUE ROBOT
BLUE. ADD BRIGHT RED LIGHTS
TO THE HEAD.

13

# AR-Lift
## The Sky Roller

Some robots are not meant to walk on solid ground. AR-Lift is made for life in the sky. It has **retractable** wings and propellers that double as hands. This air-bot can handle any **altitude**. It can refuel a jet during flight or even enter **orbit** to repair a **space station**!

## BREAK IT DOWN

JUST ABOUT ANY SUBJECT CAN BE BROKEN DOWN INTO SMALLER PARTS. LOOK FOR CIRCLES, OVALS, SQUARES, AND OTHER BASIC SHAPES THAT CAN HELP BUILD YOUR DRAWING.

**1**

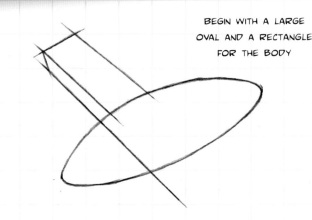

BEGIN WITH A LARGE OVAL AND A RECTANGLE FOR THE BODY

**2**

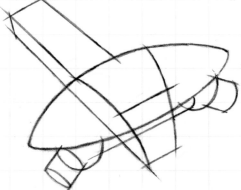

ADD CYLINDERS FOR THE ARMS

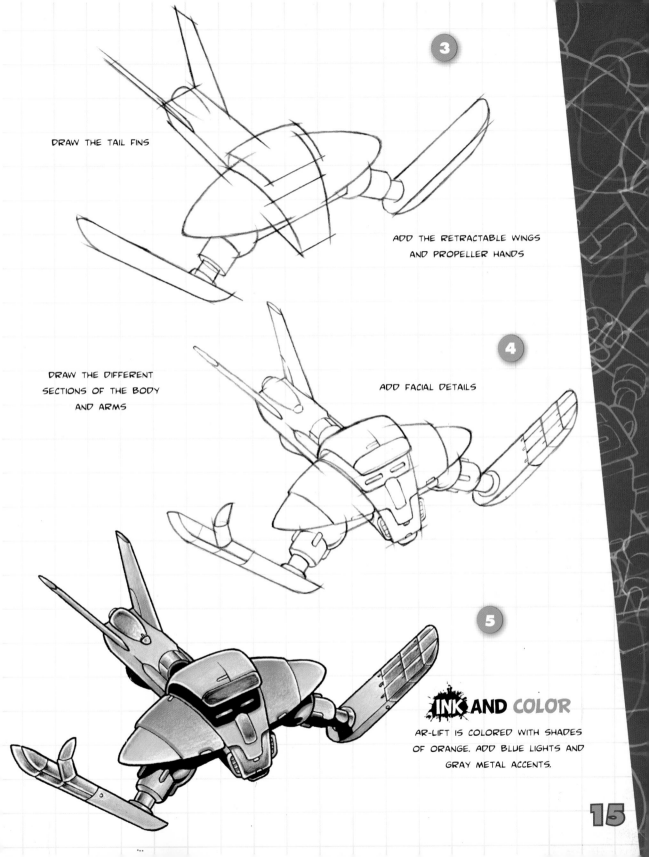

DRAW THE TAIL FINS

**3**

ADD THE RETRACTABLE WINGS
AND PROPELLER HANDS

DRAW THE DIFFERENT
SECTIONS OF THE BODY
AND ARMS

ADD FACIAL DETAILS

**4**

**5**

## INK AND COLOR

AR-LIFT IS COLORED WITH SHADES
OF ORANGE. ADD BLUE LIGHTS AND
GRAY METAL ACCENTS.

# Athletixx
## The All-Around Athlete

This programmable sports robot can do everything from throw a baseball to play hopscotch. A strong skeleton and foam shell allow you to get rough with Athletixx without worrying about serious injury. Switch to its multiplayer setting and Athletixx moves at lightning speed to play every position on a sports team!

BEGIN WITH AN OVAL-SHAPED HEAD AND A ROUNDED RECTANGLE FOR THE CHEST

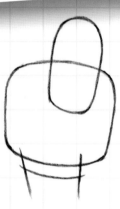

## SEE THE BIG PICTURE

WAIT TO ADD DETAILS UNTIL YOU ARE HAPPY WITH THE BASIC SHAPE OF YOUR DRAWING. YOU DON'T WANT TO SPEND TIME DETAILING A PART OF YOUR DRAWING THAT WILL BE ERASED LATER.

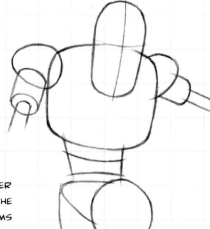

ADD THE UPPER PORTION OF THE LEGS AND ARMS

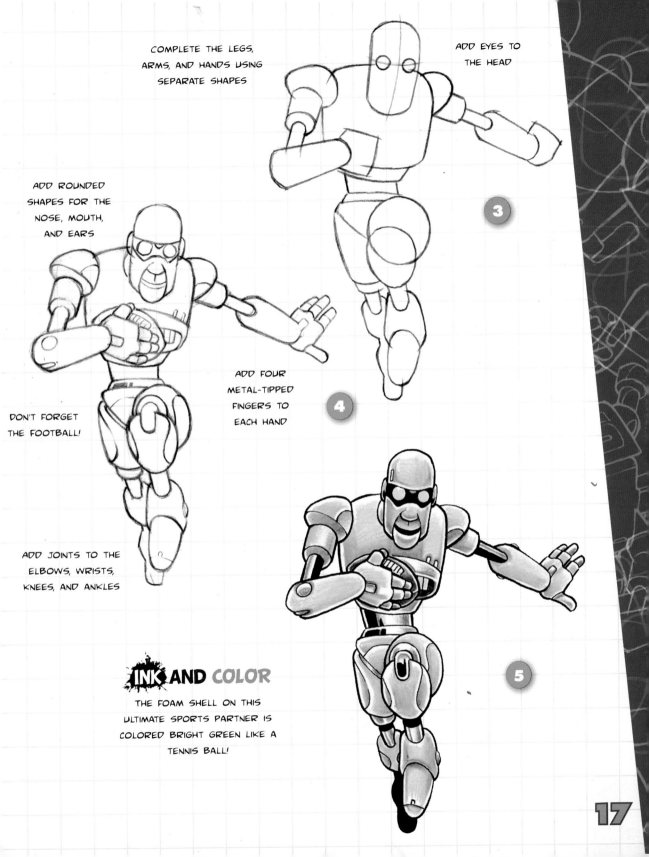

COMPLETE THE LEGS, ARMS, AND HANDS USING SEPARATE SHAPES

ADD EYES TO THE HEAD

ADD ROUNDED SHAPES FOR THE NOSE, MOUTH, AND EARS

DON'T FORGET THE FOOTBALL!

ADD FOUR METAL-TIPPED FINGERS TO EACH HAND

ADD JOINTS TO THE ELBOWS, WRISTS, KNEES, AND ANKLES

INK AND COLOR

THE FOAM SHELL ON THIS ULTIMATE SPORTS PARTNER IS COLORED BRIGHT GREEN LIKE A TENNIS BALL!

3

4

5

17

# Spike
## *The Canine Bot*

In many ways, Spike is like any security dog. It picks up scents with a **keen** nose and sprints at a speed that intruders cannot outrun. But unlike a true canine, Spike can be plugged into the wall when low on energy!

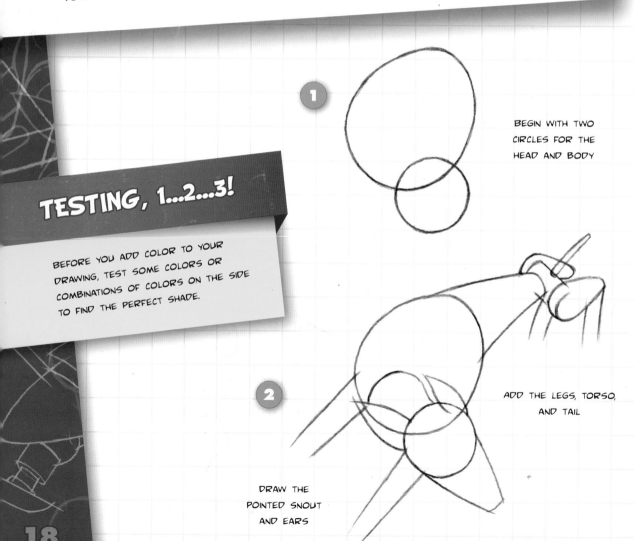

**1** BEGIN WITH TWO CIRCLES FOR THE HEAD AND BODY

## TESTING, 1...2...3!

BEFORE YOU ADD COLOR TO YOUR DRAWING, TEST SOME COLORS OR COMBINATIONS OF COLORS ON THE SIDE TO FIND THE PERFECT SHADE.

**2** ADD THE LEGS, TORSO, AND TAIL

DRAW THE POINTED SNOUT AND EARS

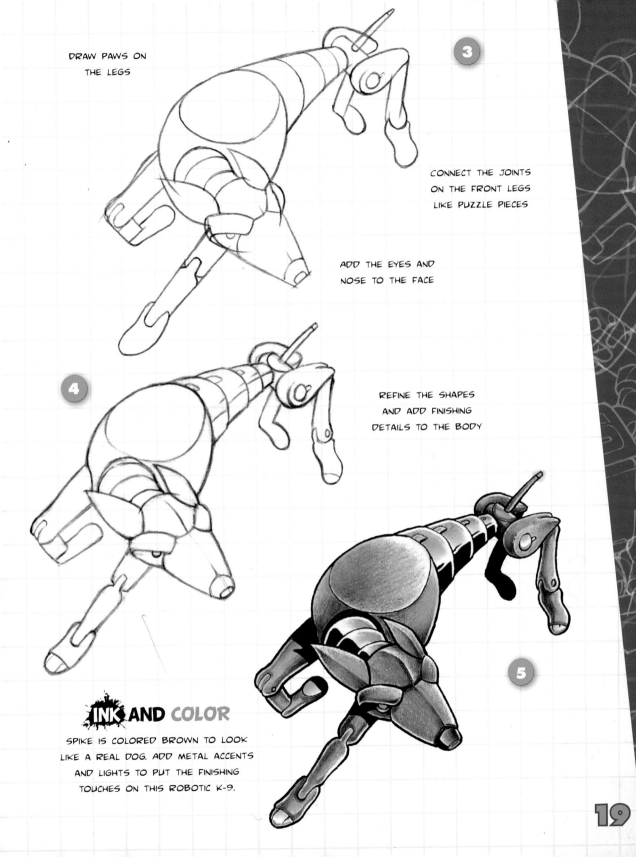

DRAW PAWS ON
THE LEGS

3

CONNECT THE JOINTS
ON THE FRONT LEGS
LIKE PUZZLE PIECES

ADD THE EYES AND
NOSE TO THE FACE

4

REFINE THE SHAPES
AND ADD FINISHING
DETAILS TO THE BODY

5

## INK AND COLOR

SPIKE IS COLORED BROWN TO LOOK
LIKE A REAL DOG. ADD METAL ACCENTS
AND LIGHTS TO PUT THE FINISHING
TOUCHES ON THIS ROBOTIC K-9.

# Bit
## The Little Digger

Bit is an **excavating** expert. This robot fits in your tool belt but is powerful enough to drill through miles of rock. Bit comes in handy when miners are trapped underground. When not acting the hero, Bit is doing valuable research beneath the **Earth's crust**.

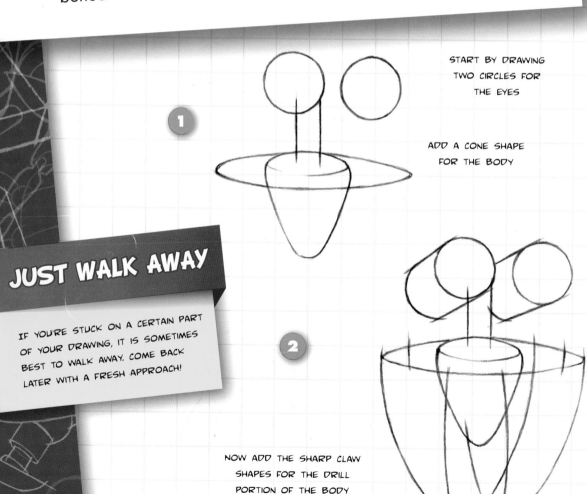

START BY DRAWING TWO CIRCLES FOR THE EYES

ADD A CONE SHAPE FOR THE BODY

NOW ADD THE SHARP CLAW SHAPES FOR THE DRILL PORTION OF THE BODY

## JUST WALK AWAY

IF YOU'RE STUCK ON A CERTAIN PART OF YOUR DRAWING, IT IS SOMETIMES BEST TO WALK AWAY. COME BACK LATER WITH A FRESH APPROACH!

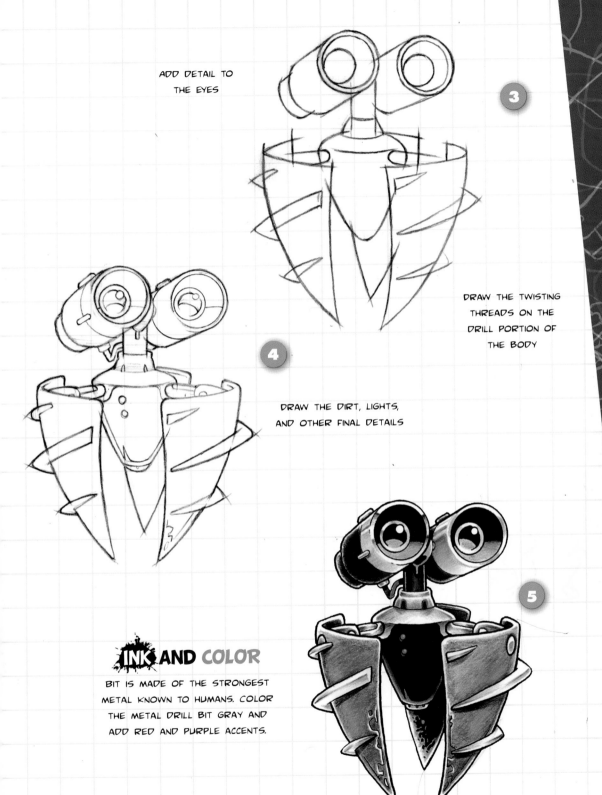

ADD DETAIL TO
THE EYES

3

DRAW THE TWISTING
THREADS ON THE
DRILL PORTION OF
THE BODY

4

DRAW THE DIRT, LIGHTS,
AND OTHER FINAL DETAILS

5

## INK AND COLOR

BIT IS MADE OF THE STRONGEST
METAL KNOWN TO HUMANS. COLOR
THE METAL DRILL BIT GRAY AND
ADD RED AND PURPLE ACCENTS.

# GLOSSARY

**altitude**—the height above sea level

**arteries**—blood vessels that carry blood from the heart to the rest of the body

**automatons**—machines that operate on their own

**demolition**—the act of tearing down buildings

**Earth's crust**—the outer layer of rock that covers the Earth; the Earth's crust is usually between 3 and 30 miles (5 and 50 kilometers) thick.

**excavating**—digging or scooping to form holes or tunnels

**humanoids**—nonhumans that take on a human form

**keen**—highly sensitive

**microscopic**—unable to be seen without the aid of a microscope

**orbit**—the path a space station follows as it moves around the Earth

**retractable**—capable of being drawn or folded back in

**rubble**—broken bits of building material

**space station**—a spacecraft that remains in orbit for long periods of time; a space station serves as a base for crew members and other spacecraft.

**tracks**—belts that wrap around wheels and grip the land as a vehicle moves

**vital**—necessary to stay alive

**wrecking ball**—a large swinging ball that is used to demolish buildings

# TO LEARN MORE

## At the Library

Bridgman, Roger. *Robot*. New York, N.Y.: DK Pub., 2004.

Masiello, Ralph. *Ralph Masiello's Robot Drawing Book*. Watertown, Mass.: Charlesbridge, 2011.

Varon, Sara. *Robot Dreams*. New York, N.Y.: First Second, 2007.

## On the Web

Learning more about robots is as easy as 1, 2, 3.

1. Go to www.factsurfer.com.

2. Enter "robots" into the search box.

3. Click the "Surf" button and you will see a list of related Web sites.

With factsurfer.com, finding more information is just a click away.

# INDEX